Sorting

Sorting by Size

by Jennifer L. Marks

Capstone press®

Mankato, Minnesota

A+ Books are published by Capstone Press,
151 Good Counsel Drive, P.O. Box 669, Mankato, Minnesota 56002.
www.capstonepress.com

1 2 3 4 5 6 12 11 10 09 08 07

Library of Congress Cataloging-in-Publication Data
Marks, Jennifer L.
    Sorting by size / by Jennifer L. Marks.
    p. cm.—(A+ books. Sorting)
    Summary: "Simple text and color photographs introduce basic concepts of sorting
by size"—Provided by publisher.
    Includes bibliographical references and index.
    ISBN-13: 978-0-7368-6740-5 (hardcover)
    ISBN-10: 0-7368-6740-6 (hardcover)
    ISBN-13: 978-0-7368-7858-6 (softcover pbk.)
    ISBN-10: 0-7368-7858-0 (softcover pbk.)
    1. Group theory—Juvenile literature. 2. Size perception—Juvenile literature. I. Title. II. Series.
QA174.5M375 2007
512'.2—dc22   2006018204

Credits

Ted Williams, designer; Charlene Deyle, photo researcher; Scott Thoms, photo editor;
    Kelly Garvin, photo stylist

Photo Credits

Capstone Press/Karon Dubke, cover, 3, 4–5, 6–7, 8, 9, 10, 11, 12–13, 14, 15, 16–17, 18, 19,
    20, 21, 22–23, 24–25 (children)
Corbis/Alan Schein Photography, 24–25 (background); Bettmann, 29
Shutterstock/Alex Hinds; 26; Anita, 27 (dolls)
SuperStock/Ron Brown, 27 (shoes)

Note to Parents, Teachers, and Librarians

The Sorting set uses color photographs and a nonfiction format to introduce readers to the key math skill of sorting. *Sorting by Size* is designed to be read aloud to a pre-reader, or to be read independently by an early reader. Images and activities encourage mathematical thinking in early readers and listeners. The book encourages further learning by including the following sections: Table of Contents, Facts about Size, Read More, Internet Sites, and Index. Early readers may need assistance using these features.

The author dedicates this book to Mark Sundell of New Ulm, Minnesota.

Table of Contents

Size It Up!

Check out the different sizes of balls, blocks, and beads. How can we sort them?

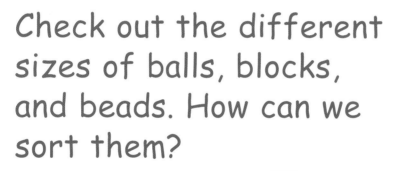

5

First, let's put alike things together to make sets. We have a set of beads, a set of blocks, and a set of balls.

Now, let's sort some sets by size!

Big and Small

From big and round to teeny-tiny, beads come in many sizes.

We can sort them by size. Make a set of small beads and a set of big beads.

Building blocks can be sorted by size too. Try sorting sets of big, medium, and small blocks.

These balls are sorted by size. Which set is big and which is small?

Long and Short

Now let's sort by long and short. Put dolls with long hair on the top shelf. A set of short-haired dolls sits on the bottom shelf.

Long to short, these pieces of sidewalk chalk are sorted by size.

Soft, cozy scarves can be sorted long to short.

Thick and Thin

Sorting birthday presents is a fun way to sort by size. You can stack your presents, thick to thin.

Mmmm! Let's sort cookies. Stack the thin cookies in one pile. Put the thick cookies in another.

A bunch of books can be sorted by size too. Sort them out, thick to thin.

Wide and Narrow

It's fun to doodle and write with markers of all sizes.

Let's sort them into sets
by size, narrow and wide.

Lying this way, the girls have sorted their hair ribbons from wide to narrow.

Tall and Short

You and your friends
are all different heights.
Sort yourselves from
short to tall!

YOU MUST
BE THIS TALL
←

Sorting by Size in the Real World

You can spot sorting in all kinds of places. Let's look at some of the ways people sort by size in the real world.

In toolboxes and in hardware stores, you can find nails and screws sorted by size.

Toy stores sometimes sort toys by size, like these nesting dolls. They are sorted big to small.

Bowling alleys sort their shoes by size. Workers can easily find the right size shoe for each bowler.

Facts about Size

- The thickest ice ever recorded is in Antarctica. It measures nearly 3 miles (4.8 kilometers) thick. Antarctica is a continent made up almost entirely of snow and ice.

- A Chinese woman named Xhu Haizen is the shortest woman in the world. By age 19, she stood just 2.5 feet (.76 meters) tall.

- The smallest mammal in the world is a bat from Thailand. The hog-nosed bat is less than 2 inches (5 centimeters) long. It is smaller than many insects and snails.

- The blue whale is the largest animal to ever have lived on the planet. It is bigger than even the largest dinosaur. Blue whales can weigh as much as 190 tons (172 metric tons).

- The narrowest house in the world is located in Amsterdam, the Netherlands. It is slightly more than 6 feet (1.8 meters) wide.

- The Nile River in Egypt is the longest river in the world. It is 4,145 miles (6,671 kilometers) long. The Roe River in Missouri is the shortest river in the world. It is only 200 feet (61 meters) long.

- The tallest man ever to live was Robert Pershing Wadlow. Born in 1918, he grew to a height of 8 feet, 11.1 inches (2.7 meters). You can see a life-size bronze statue of Wadlow in his hometown of Alton, Illinois.

Glossary

cozy (KOH-zee)—soft and comfortable

life-size (LIFE-size)—the same size as the real thing; a life-size statue of someone is the same size as that person.

mammal (MAM-uhl)—a warm-blooded animal with a backbone

medium (MEE-dee-uhm)—middle; something that is a medium size is in between big and small sizes.

narrow (NA-roh)—not broad or wide

set (SET)—a group of alike things

ton (TUHN)—a unit of weight equal to 2,000 pounds or 907.2 kilograms

weigh (WAY)—to have a certain weight; weight is a measurement of how heavy a person or thing is.

Read More

Boothroyd, Jennifer. *Grouping.* First Step Nonfiction. Minneapolis: LernerClassroom, 2007.

Faulkner, Keith. *The Tallest, Shortest, Longest, Greenest, Brownest Animal in the Jungle!* New York: Dutton Children's Books, 2002.

Pluckrose, Henry Arthur. *Sorting and Sets.* Let's Explore. North Mankato, Minn.: Sea to Sea, 2006.

Internet Sites

FactHound offers a safe, fun way to find Internet sites related to this book. All of the sites on FactHound have been researched by our staff.

Here's how:

1. Visit *www.facthound.com*

2. Choose your grade level.

3. Type in this book ID **0736867406** for age-appropriate sites. You may also browse subjects by clicking on letters, or by clicking on pictures and words.

4. Click on the **Fetch It** button.

FactHound will fetch the best sites for you!

Index